THE NIGGER FROM THE BLACK LAGOON

SHANE WILLIAMS

Copyright © 2024 Shane Williams

ISBN:
978-1-952874-92-5 (paperback)
978-1-952874-93-2 (hardback)
978-1-952874-94-9 (ebook)

All rights reserved.
No part of this publication may be reproduced, stored in a retrieval system, or transmitted in any form or by any means – electronic, mechanical, photocopy, recording, scanning, or other – except for brief quotations in critical reviews or articles, without the prior written permission of the publisher.

Published by:

OB OMNIBOOK Co.

OMNIBOOK CO.
99 Wall Street, Suite 118
New York, NY 10005
USA
+1-866-216-9965
www.omnibook.org

For e-book purchase: Kindle on Amazon, Barnes and Noble
Book purchase: Amazon.com, Barnes & Noble, and
www.omnibook.org

Omnibook titles may be purchased in bulk for educational, business, fund-raising, or sales promotional use. For more information please e-mail admin@omnibook.org

The Nigger from the Black Lagoon

Is being in America a death zone? I thought it was a place of freedom, freedom of speech, a place of living a healthy life. It seems now to be a place of judging race, and skin color. Has America always been about that? I guess if you're black, this has been forever.

Black people are a minority race. Are other minority races in the same situation? They are supposed to have come to America because they wanted to be free and accepted for their skin color, race, and culture. They also sought a place to work, get an education, a job, and raise their family, so they chose to come to America.

Lately, America hasn't seemed like a place of the free, has it ever been? It now seems like an unstable, death hell hole, a place for devilish evil people. America is like hell right now, I've never seen hell and ain't gonna never see it. Homelessness, rent hikes, mortgage hikes, hikes at the gas pumps, people starving, babies are now a high crime issue, gun issue, guns in the wrong hands issue, people getting killed by guns everyday issue, Congress doesn't give a shit issue.

Washington D.C., the White House, is the capital place of bill signing to make changes all across every city and state in America. That's the place where the shit starts and where it can stop, all it takes is a couple of votes and signing a damn piece of paper, that's all folks.

Oh my God, you can get killed in America for being black, has it always been this way for black people getting killed?

You can get killed shopping for groceries, at a pharmacy, doctor's office, shopping mall, kids can get killed for sitting in school, getting an education.

To get killed in America because a racist person came into your community to kill you because you're black, this can also happen through getting pulled over and stopped by a racist cop. It turns into a wrestling match with another black person, young or old, dead on the ground, whether they were choked out, knee on back of neck, or just shot for making the wrong move.

I know white people are having it tough as well, and they also have their personal issues, but out of any minority in America, blacks seem to really have it tougher. Besides racist people coming to visit us in our community to kill us, let's not forget black on black crime.

Why do black people kill each other every day and every night in this place called the ghetto? Well, the ghetto is a low-income community, or even the projects, AKA public housing. There are good, every day, 9 to 5 hard-working black people in the war zone AKA the ghetto, fighting every day trying to move out. But remember, soldiers in any war may or may not make it out. That war, I guess, it depends on how and what, or how big or much you're doing to make it out. When I use the word racist, I'm not pointing any race or color of people out; anyone can be a racist. It depends on their level of hatred and how black their heart is. When guns get into the hands of a person who may be a racist, or have mental illness, or a person who just has hatred towards different races and feels that their race is being replaced or overtaken by other races, their sick mind tells them to take a stand and do something about it. So, they purchase a gun from an 'I don't give a shit' gun dealer and just travel or walk to wherever their sick, crazy, hateful mind tells them to go. But remember, everyone who is doing this in America is not mentally ill; some or most are quite aware of what they are about to do, because all these shooters have a website or a YouTube channel, and they're speaking about what they are about to do. So, parents, if you see this shit on your teenager's internet about killing people or a hit list to kill other races, including blacks, or kids in a school, or killing people because of their religion, please pick up the phone and call the police. You've just found out that your teenager is a monster and doesn't need to walk the streets or be around people anymore. Parents need to take a stand. Also, any minority or black person can get killed just for walking through a racist person's community, which is the wrong community if you're black. Many black people have gotten killed just for walking, minding their business, through somewhere they maybe should not have been. They were killed because that racist neighborhood saw them as a threat.

Gun sellers and gun dealers, please check out the person you're about to sell a gun to. Ask for ID, copy that person's address, Social Security number, and name, please. Getting a gun in the war zone AKA the ghetto, black people's neighborhoods, is like finding a liquor store on every corner or a drug dealer on every corner; it's very, very easy. Black people, don't you think that the racist people are not seeing the streaming TV, cable news, and not reading newspapers? They are. They see and hear blacks killing each other, day in, day out, in every ghetto across 52 cities and states.

Ok, so you're only going to protest and come together when a racist person kills you, and not protest when you kill each other? You think Congress can fix black on black crime? Think about it, that's bullshit. Change your mentality and your way of thinking, black people.

Ok, who has ever faced racism? Well, as a black man or black woman, I know I have. Anyone else? Raise your hand. Any high-class rich blacks or any educated blacks ever faced racism at any time in your life? Maybe in college, what about during your acting career, or modeling career, sports career? Any kind of racism if you're a high-class or middle-class black person in America, look me in my eyes and say no, I never faced any kind of racism.

Look me in my black freaking face right now and say no, you've never faced racism as a black person. You are a damn lie if you say no, never. I don't believe you because unfortunately, racism is a part of America, and sadly, it will always be a part of America. I see skin color, race, and different cultures; I try to look at everyone as a human being with acceptance. I should hope others see me and feel the same way also. Parents who have not yet begun to explain the silly sickness going on in America, now is the time to really talk to your kids. Let them know there are crazy, mentally ill, racist people of all ages walking, commuting side by side with us every day, waiting for their moment.

And that sick person, or racist, or mentally ill person may want to kill you just because you look different, or because your skin color is different, or your race, culture, or religion is different. Teach them what to do if one of these bad, evil people come. Call for help. If you have a mobile phone, believe me, people, if there is ever a time to talk to your kids, it's right now. Tell them how to conduct themselves if a bad police officer pulls them over in their car. Many young minorities have lost their lives just for a police traffic stop. Also, grown adults have to look around more, be more aware of who is in your surroundings, regardless of what color or race they are. Look everywhere and be more careful, and also make sure your mobile or cell phone stays working.

Also, could it be that someone can just pick up a gun, a machine gun, or an AR-15 rifle and kill others just because their life is upside down and jacked up? And maybe because they hate themselves to the highest degree, they hate themselves so much that they end up killing others. We all have two viruses, COVID-19 and guns in the wrong hands. I'm just a plain author, not a fortune teller, I'm ordinary just like you. I can't see any further than my hands in front of my face. Therefore, I cannot write and say things will get better. I don't know, maybe, maybe not. We can only hope and believe that it will.

Besides all the massacre shootings in America, also let's beware of all the terrorist groups. They could be planning another attack on Americans. Don't forget 9/11. The difference between a massacre shooter and a terrorist is that a terrorist doesn't see skin color. They just want to kill Americans, period. If you live in or are from America, you're dead to them, bottom line.

No one wants to get killed and murdered from a crime, from a massacre shooting, a terrorist attack, or even from COVID. People in the world have their own way they would like to leave this earth, a way that each imagines. But when you're killed, you've been robbed of that.

So, who do we go to for answers? A pastor, your priest, adults are confused and scared. Children are confused and also scared. No one seems to have an answer about what's going on in America, with massacre shootings, crimes, racial shootings, every day in communities across America. I wish I had the answer and could say things are going to get better, but I cannot say that, because I don't know, like you don't know. I guess as long as there are bad people in the world who practice being evil and doing evil acts, we mix around with these kinds of people every day in society and they look so normal with a smile on their face. But inside their hearts is a deep black hole. So unfortunately, these evil acts may never stop. We can only hope and pray that it will stop.

Believe whether you believe or not,
Believe whether you want to or not,
Believe if you're feeling up, believe if you're feeling down,
Believe on a sunny day, believe on a rainy day,
Believe if you're broke and have no money,
Believe if you have no food, believe if you're homeless,

Believe if you're sad, believe if you're happy,
Believe if you can't see a way, believe if you don't have a way.

Believe if you're deaf, and can't hear,
Believe if you're blind and can't see.
Believe if you're a cripple or a handicap and can't walk or stand,
Believe no matter who hates you.
Believe no matter who's talking behind your back,
Believe if you have no friends,
Believe even if you have enemies,
Believe if you have no job and might be seeking a job,
Believe if you have a lot on your mind and don't want to be bothered.
Believe no matter how many loved ones passed away.

Believe even if you feel like committing suicide and you want to end your life,
Believe if you're not feeling well.
Believe if you have a physical disease,
Believe if people are stepping on you,
Believe if people don't like the color of your skin.
Believe even if someone or people are being racist against you, believe if you're ugly,
Believe if you're fat and don't look as good as the next person.
Believe because you have a good heart,
Believe that this messed up world will get better one day.
I hope both you and I are still around to see it.

Believe even if you're a drug addict,
Believe if you're an alcoholic,
Believe if you're a killer and stop killing people, believe if you're a rapist and stop raping women.
Believe if you have dreams that they will come true,
Believe, young people in school and in college, that you can make things right in this world one day. Believe if you can't pay your rent, believe if you can't pay your mortgage,
Believe if you can't pay any bills at all,
Believe one day that you can.

Believe even if someone made you mad,
Believe if you're sad,
Believe and keep the faith,
Believe even if you don't own much in this world,
Believe and keep a smile on your face.

Believe even if you doubt,
Believe even if you've had bad luck in your life,
Believe if you ain't never had any luck,
Believe anything is possible,
Also believe that you're a force that's unstoppable.
Believe, believe, believe,
And you shall receive, receive, receive.

Do you believe, believe you can climb the highest mountains,
Whatever you wish for, believe,
Whatever you desire, believe,
Whatever you dream, believe,
Whatever your goals are, believe,

Whatever breath you inhale, believe.

Believe if you have a long walk,
Believe on whatever journey you take,
Ok, things have been so bad in your life that you can't believe,
Believe step by step, make it a prerogative,
Believe you can leap and jump,
More higher than the next person,
Believe you can be more smarter and wiser than the next person.

Believe you are tall, believe you can stand tall,
Even if you're short,
Hey, why not?
Believe you can touch the stars,
Believe you can reach the moon,
Believe you can touch the sun and get a suntan from the scorching hot rays,
Believe you're a rocket going through the clouds,
Believe you're an angel sitting on a cloud,
Playing a beautiful song with a harp,
Believe you're an eagle flying over all the oceans and seas,
Or like a bird floating in an airy cool breeze,
Your wings spread out wide, floating over the water high tides.
Believe you're standing taller than the tallest building,
Believe you're taller than any mountain,
Believe you're bigger than any bridges, believe you're wonderful,

Believe you're magnificent, believe you're special, believe you're a king,
Believe you're a queen,
Believe you're special, believe you're a prince, believe you're a princess,
Maybe one day soon you will be.
Believe how many times you want,
Believe because you love it, believe like it's your best.

I believe, do you believe? Should we believe? Is there anything worth believing in? Believe we are a piece of art, colors painting on a wall, painted different colors, beautiful colors,
Of all races, light colors, dark colors,
Bright colors, happy colors, feeling good colors, loving colors.

Believe we all are colorful rainbow, mixed with peaceful colors, running through our spirits and souls, all these colors are leading in different directions, positive directions, the right directions.
We all are sliding up and down and around and around like a rollercoaster towards joy and happiness.

Husbands shooting and killing their wives, boyfriends shooting and killing their girlfriends, and vice versa. Can we still believe, although people's minds have become violent, racist, and determined and confused? Calibers, AR-15 Rifles, sure guns are in the wrong hands. People, I'm afraid to say these violent gun crimes are going to continue, and gun shop dealers are going to continue to sell guns to the wrong people.

No one cares, the government, the president, politicians, democrats, and republicans, it's very sad. I'm mad, I'm not glad, everyone is scared and complaining, even your mom and dad. How these senseless worldwide crimes are ending up with innocent people in a body bag, and with a toe tag, dag dag, I'm mad, I can't brag, things are too bad. No criminals care about raising the white flag, there's no surrender. But can I? Can we? Still believe? I believed when nobody supported me, I believed when nobody loved me, I believed when I was hungry, I believed when I, yes me, was homeless, didn't have anywhere to sleep at nights. I believed even when I, yes me, thought about suicide. Yes, this life is full of pressures.

No, you can't measure the pressure, when it rains it pours. Believe in a storm, believe in your poem inside you, feeling warm, through life you've been ripped apart and torn, believe I sworn, after all your struggles and rejections in life you've been reborn. Believe in the rapture, look to hear the horn, the trumpets caught up in the clouds, to meet our God, the Almighty one who controls our minds, life, spirit, and soul. What I'm saying is believing is the goal, be strong and tough, don't fold, as we all continue to troll through life. Being bold is a mold inside of us, worth more than gold. Our knees get shaky at times in this world so cold, believing and keeping the faith seems like all the grip to hold, regardless if you're young or old.

As a black man or black woman, or Negro, who is your hero? People in the past and present, who stood on the front line, Like Martin Luther King, Malcolm X, Jesse Jackson, and Rev. Al Sharpton, have also put his life on the line through the years. Men of voices and action. Racism and black on black crimes are still painful contractions. Seems like there's no change from past actions, just reactions. Let's all face the facts and stop pretending. Things are all that, and black people are collapsing from injustice, killings, murders, and everyday crime, because there's no satisfaction.

No, I'm not rapping, hand clapping, toe tapping, nor am I laughing. It's hard to believe when people only look to the color of your skin when you're a black man. "White is right" is the old saying, although there are poor whites struggling, and poor whether you're white or black, doing the hustle thing. Let us use our biggest muscle, that's our brain, maintain please! Don't go insane, rich people don't give a damn, their main concern is their fortune and fame.

Big or small, do you hear what I'm saying y'all? Believe you have the toughness, believe you have the roughness without the fussin' and cussin'. We all look better when we're blushing.

So much is going on in the world now, now people are saying, what's going on? What is this? What's happening? It's serious, I'm curious, we all are getting delirious, sometimes furious, period.

The Nigger from the Black Lagoon

I'm an Author, a writer, a cigarette lighter, as I write and write, things become brighter. My height gets higher and higher, I'm on a mission, like a surgeon, deep incision. If I'm not writing, I'd rather be sitting on a park bench feeding the pigeons, stay away from people that make you frown, they act like a clown, they're always around, waiting to laugh in your face when you fall down. People don't want to see you make it, they'd rather see you break it, believe me, when you get your chance, don't fake it. Being real is solid steel, anything else is no frill.

I'm disappointed in myself, I dated a crackhead bitch, and she loved being a bitch, with every inch of her breath. She was a short, big butt witch, 5.2 feet high, she came to me first saying I have nice big eyes, I haven't heard anything much nicer in my life, I was surprised, of what I heard, word up. This old crackhead bitch had a big jelly butt, that was my weakness, she said she was half black and half Puerto Rican. I saw her no good father, he had curly hair, skin so white, looked like he been bleaching. We've dated, we started creeping, in and out of my apartment, I let her stay, in my bed she lay, we've played, it was me she betrayed. The relationship we've so called had, was cutting closer than a fade, although her mother got her on crack, it was her bed she made, her choice with me, try to stir her in a better direction, she had it made. She relapsing, around me over and over, in and out of drug programs, never staying clean during her street crack mission, she became determined and bolder. She would be on her crack mission for weeks, coming in my apartment, with a fish and sardine body odor, I knew at some point this be over, I couldn't stand her stealing from me, damn her, I cram to understand her. She laughed at how she robbed people, she was evil.

When she relapsed, she was a low down dirty dick-sucking bitch, I tried to believe I could change this bitch mischief friction, she was a bad influence, 6 years older than me, I was 47 she was 53. She walked around my house with her gown on, with nothing underneath, I had her bent over in my bed doggy style many times with my curled up feet. Orgasm was loud like a block party in the street, I said "oh," "oh," "oh," "aww," "aww," "aww," "oh," "oh," "oh," I felt good inside her. it was satisfaction, very relaxation.

I filled her up to the rim, she took a tissue and tried to stop the leaking, ran to the bathroom, wiped herself with soap and a rag. I thought to myself, "Dang, is this going to last?" Banging her big juicy butt from the back, doggy style, smacking noises back and forth, I had to reach my peak. Hey, she was living with me for free, so it wasn't long before she got dressed and went back to the streets. I got sick of that. I like all sizes of women, skinny or fat, being with her I realized I was better than that. All she ever did was rob the streets for thousands, with her money wasn't a problem, that's word son. I've been better off stroking off using my palm and thumb, man I was done, I dated a crumb.

She showed me her world, one she loved so much, it wasn't me, it was her crack, drug dealers, and glass dick, aka crack pipe. She was popular around her crack friends, who just used and abused her. When she was sober, she acted as if she never knew them. Her drug dealers knew me from hanging with her, and they would walk past and say to me, "What's up, bro? We'd rather deal with you than her." I said, "Nah, this is not my thing." I walked away, knowing things had to change.

The only thing she taught me was how to roll up and smoke weed. Seeing her smoke crack was really disgusting to me, and the smell was horrible. Seeing all these crackheads made me nauseous. Drug dealers, young and old, were always on the lookout for the cops, being cautious. A serious drug addiction is an easy cash flow absorption.

Therefore, last year, 2021, it was over and done with this dark room relationship. It was the two worst years of my life, it wasn't worth anything, not worth the trouble. Never, not once, had I ever asked her for a crack hit. I stood firm, my inner structure was tough like leather. My mental function just had enough of all the mess.

All I've been through, I'm still gifted and blessed, it was all a test, and I passed with flying colors. I was left on this earth by a strong, thriving, and struggling mother. Lord, rest her soul. Thinking of her not being here anymore makes me feel cold, somehow her spirit still touches my soul, but every day I continue to get old. I still believe because I am a believer, my gift of writing will uplift you and cool down your fever. I am more honest than Ward Cleaver and the Beaver. In the Bronx, New York, for 7 years, I was a parking attendant in a rat den, a dirty, nasty parking garage, a small French fry, I was stepped on. People coming in didn't speak, transit workers, correction officers, mailmen, managers, supervisors, caseworkers, whoever, I really hated that job. I felt and was treated like a slob. There was a dark, bald-headed guy who came in every morning wearing nice suits, I saw his shiny badge, he was a cop, a detective, and he never ever spoke, I thought that was hectic. If only those same people could see me now and see that I was gifted, an author, a writer was my selection, they'd read my book and be like, "Wow, I now can feel this man's pain and perfection." Then they might say, "He is a good writer, is he coming out with a book collection?"

They might also say I wished I walked by and spoke to this man and showed some affection. I've been writing since 1985, at age 13, 37 years, I don't need those people's election or correction. I wasn't on their 9-5 level, so I felt their rejections, and to me, that's the worst injections. Oh, excuse me, TikTok, ticktock, time is passing, let me stop talking about my own issues, as the tall hand moves round and round to catch the little hand on the clock. I hope me or no one catches the chickenpox, another virus, another plague. I think we have to continue to get vaccinated, yes, you and I both hate it, but it's better to be safe than sorry. Life is worth more than the drop of a quarter. I used to live in New York City, where young kids forming gangs were randomly robbing old people, so I moved to Florida. How can you see your surroundings becoming violent, and you sit there and do nothing? Don't be dumb, be smart, your intelligence and awareness are your art, developed in your mind and heart.

Also, wisdom please. Add that word to your cart, the sharpness of any dart, even though I'm not the right skin color, I can still be a good lover. I'm being myself, not any other or another. I'm the only child. I don't have a sister or brother. I was raised a bastard and was raised by a single mother who in 2014 died at 59 and lay in a casket. She didn't ask for this, no one asks for this, it just happened. A man can carry a lot of hurt in his basket. I think about her every day, forever and ever it would never be past tense. She always said men are like sitting ducks, that's so tragic. Dying is no magic trick, it's not sarcastic. Do you see me laughing? Shut your mouth quick, or you might get your ass kicked. I'm not violent. I don't be cursing. I write my verses on pages for all the ages. Some men don't have any get-up. They are slaves trapped in their own cages. Only you have the keys to your mind and heart, to go in and out of. Let's thank the Lord above. Okay, I give rough encouragement. I give you a push and a shove. Maybe then you can believe, begin to swim, begin to paddle, begin to see, begin to agree.

No need for debate, dreams come true, just have patience, keep running and racing towards it. My words are about elevation, recreation, stay focused, no hocus pocus. Let your creation develop mental inflation. My words are real and original, you can carve them in the pavement. Don't do that to yourself. Break away from that inner enslavement. When I was a teenager, no one believed in me. They didn't think I would be anything, but I knew one day I would rise higher than any tree. See, in my mind, there were no ifs, ands, or buts, or maybes. Haters are like parasites. They eat right through you. Regardless, be no one else but you. Do what you do. See? I have a vision. I can see right through you, hating on me. Well, that's common. I've experienced that, but I'm flying high over the mountains, and I'm thirsty from my verses. I'm looking for a water fountain. You can be the same way. Have an input of determination with no delay. Do you hear what I say? Okay.

If someone spits in your face, still believe you're going to make it. If someone doesn't want to stand next to you or touch you, still believe you can make it. If someone doesn't like the culture or race you're in, still believe. Believing is like a sledgehammer; it can knock down any tough door of struggle. Keep banging and hitting that door of struggle over and over again until you see a hole. That hole is a breakthrough. When you see that hole, look at the sunlight bursting through. That sunlight is your true essence.

It took a long time, but I didn't give up. Now, you're an angel in the clouds, or maybe like a spoiled child, running with speed. Your feet are now on the accelerator. An unstoppable force is what you wanted. Now continue to follow that sunlight and stay on course. Don't get swiped, keep your head up high, and your tears wiped. Remember, every day is another day. When you wake up with joy, you can say, "Oh Lord, thank you. I found a new way."

Always be the same, yesterday, today, and always. Never change who you are, except for the better. This is what I do. I keep punching the bag, building my muscles, continuing to fight and strive, staying alive. Nowadays, it seems like everything is a hustle. This is no bullshit. My words are nitty-gritty and hardcore, not soft and squeezable like a pair of titties. The weight of life can smash you, outcast you, and your enemies wish for your demise, hoping they outlast you. Keep your enemies close to you, not behind you in the rearview. At the same time, continue to seek prosperity by reading and believing in my teachings.

I've been writing for 37 years. I'm your art and your author, a masterpiece to be hung up in your gallery. I've had hand-me-downs, and I've accepted food from food pantries. Working as a parking attendant was a tragedy, not much of a salary. Connecting the dots, trying to make ends meet, I was worth more than a lot, while people looked down on me like a dirty penny.

We all are living risky lives, making risky choices, taking risky decisions, and facing risky chances. We're here today and gone tomorrow in this thin, fragile life we live. We can't foresee anything, clueless about the unknown. Sometimes our knees buckle from fear, unsure of which direction to turn, whether to stay, run, or hide. Wipe your tears and still believe because time is our enemy. That's why some people sometimes don't wear a watch. A calendar is our enemy, days and months are our enemies. It's like we're all on a train riding with no brakes, and death is the motorman. There are no local stops, just gliding and speeding fast through dark tunnels, one after another, until each man and woman reaches old age, their demise. That's the last stop on the train. Wipe your tears and still believe. So yes, love, be happy, enjoy everything life has to offer to the fullest. But remember, life is only a train ride, moving through the tunnels day in and day out.

In 1985, at the age of 13, as a Black young American teenager, I was given a wonderful gift. Thank you, Jesus, for birthing my talented writing skills and for the birth of an author. While I was physically born in 1972, it was in 1985 that my writing skills truly came to life. I've experienced both tears and cheers in my life. Throughout my life, I've had to wipe away many tears. Some were visible, streaming down my face, while others I managed to hide. The deepest tears I shed were those from within, the inner tears of a broken heart. I was an underdog to many. Nobody believed in me or thought I would amount to anything significant. Therefore, I never shared with anyone this wonderful gift I was nurturing, raising, and pampering like a little baby. I guess I didn't want anyone to laugh at me or make fun of me if I revealed my passion. So, for all these years, I kept it to myself.

Now, at the age of 49, almost 50, like a plane stalled on the runway, I have finally taken off. People are starting to notice. This is my second book, a testament to the fact that I also had to wipe my tears and still believe.

I've been down and out, I've been nothing until this very day, every day I still feel like nothing, trying to get something. Believe naturally or spiritually, stay on your knees praying or standing up praying, keeping the faith, that's an order, no exemption. Did I mention keeping the faith will take you through this world of torture? There is no flip side, stay wise, be wise, or get wise. Keep digging deep inside, and one day you'll be surprised at what you can accomplish. Whatever goal you desire will be your prize. Be like a kite gliding high through the skies, and don't look back, stay on track. Be the aggressor, don't accept anything less. Conquer, maintain, stay in school, go to college, fill your brain with knowledge. Stay grounded and original, be visual. I know it's difficult because things are so miserable.

Regardless of your struggles, regardless of how many loved ones have passed away, regardless of racism, regardless of who may not like your skin color, which is the interior of hate in America, regardless if no one loves you, regardless of who's talking behind your back, regardless if people think they are better than you, regardless of who looks down on you, regardless if you're not rich or don't have a lot of money, regardless if you don't have many worldly possessions, wipe your tears.

Regardless if you have many enemies, regardless if your refrigerator is half empty or completely empty, regardless if you're hungry or homeless, regardless if you're stressed out, regardless if you're happy, regardless if you're sad, regardless if you're mad, regardless if you're glad, regardless if you're handicapped or crippled, wipe your tears.

Regardless of how many downfalls you may have in your life, regardless of how many mistakes you've made in life, regardless of how many bad choices you've made in life, wipe your tears and still believe.

Regardless if you're an ugly person, wipe your tears.

Regardless if your figure doesn't look as good as the next person, wipe your tears. Maybe you drive a beat-down car and everyone else drives an updated, beautiful car, wipe your tears.

Regardless if everyone's clothes look better than yours, your clothes may be worn out and raggedy, and your shoes may be run over, wipe your tears.

Regardless of how tough times are right now, regardless of how many viruses and diseases are developing right now, like COVID and monkeypox, wipe your tears and still believe.

Regardless of all your fears, it's okay to have fears, just don't let them control your life. Regardless if you have an illness or sickness, wipe your tears.

You're waiting for the rain to stop and there are cloudy skies, waiting for the storm to pass with loud thunder and lightning. Through those clouds, you're waiting for the sun to burst through so you can feel the sun's rays and search for better days. Wipe your tears and still believe.

Day or night, night or day, wipe your tears because, knowing in your heart, everything is going to be okay soon. Wipe your tears.

Maybe you just got out of a bad marriage or got divorced or regardless if you just broke up from a bad relationship or someone broke your heart, wipe your tears and still believe.

Waiting for rough seas and oceans to become calmer, wipe your tears.

You don't see your shadow reflecting on rivers and lakes, don't worry because the sun is not shining yet, wipe your tears and still believe.

Through all the fog and gloom, wipe your tears. Feeling labor pains and contracting from the baby in the womb, don't wipe your tears, those are tears of joy.

Whether you're a man or a woman and have doubts because your mental state is wavy and not altogether, and maybe you want to commit suicide, don't do it. Call someone and wipe your tears and still believe. That's not you who wants to take your life, that's the devil because he knows you're special and there are great things awaiting, don't let the devil rob you of that.

Regardless, listen to good thoughts and hold on, be strong, because the journey is long. Don't give up, and wipe your tears, because you and I are only human, mortal not immortal, with one life to live. To my readers, remember, tomorrow is not promised to any of us. But wipe your tears and still believe.

This world that we live in is part of selfishness, hatefulness, wickedness, evilness, sinfulness, and greediness, with no sharing, no caring, single mothers bearing children, some fatherless, some motherless, others family less. Wipe your tears and still believe.

Disease after disease, inflation after inflation, nation after nation, season after season, year after year, tear after tear, then we ask, when will this nightmare end? Wipe your tears and still believe.

As I mentioned in my first book "Gray Hairs in the Mirror," aging sucks, dying sucks, racism sucks, and life is like a large pail of vomit. Whether you believe what I just said or not, wipe your tears and still believe.

The things that should define us as people are love, kindness, wisdom, smartness, and intelligence. It seems like hatred in this world has blossomed over many years, becoming our only evidence of past and present bitterness. Wipe your tears and still believe.

All races of people are like a colorful rainbow, bringing inner warm feeling, excitement, and goosebumps on our skin, just like standing close to a beautiful sunset over the horizon. It's like an autumn breeze blowing brown leaves around in the air, turning and spinning. In that one split moment, we forget all our worries and cares. I hope all my readers can see things from my view. Wipe your tears and still believe.

Goals, dreams, hopes, like flames of fire burning inside your heart's desire, people see you and admire, your motivation, determination spreading elevation, with this, a man can create their wildest creation. At your own pace, and we've won the race, competition hurts like a punch in the face. Have patience, do it yourself, learn to tie up your own shoelace, bear the wear and tear. No, don't say it's not fair, no, don't swear. Yes, this life can kick your derriere, fight and stand tall, like a giant long claw grizzly bear. Keep love in our hearts, with a lot of love to share. Yes, tempers flare, because you can't seem to be getting anywhere, with all your grinding. Seems like you may be going backwards, rewinding. Is it all about timing? Digging deeper in your heart and mind, searching and finding, the cause or reason. Give applause, waking up with breath still in our bodies is so pleasing, season after season, is more time to keep believing.

Ok, so every man is born with a time to live and die. Some people like to deceive, don't ask why, because of Adam and Eve. At the beginning of time, they sinned against God. Now every man is feeling God's wrath and the whip of his rod. Every struggle, every hustle, with the sweat of our brow, we must all carry the weight and flex our muscle. Life has many regrets, but stay in check, stay correct, continue to be your best, nothing less. I know it's stress, not knowing what to face next. To all this apply, think high thoughts like the blue color of the sky. Don't rely on others, because all the doubters will let you down then you might cry. Just say you know you can do it and slice your own piece of pie. Remember to wipe your tears and still believe. Top of Form

Lying down on an island beach, under the moon and stars late at night, in a daze, maybe you just got engaged. You and your spouse or partner hear the waves, see the moonlight glittering over each wave from the cool breeze. Thinking, meditating, dreaming, your soul floating, spirit elevating, with clear thoughts and relaxing. Smiling, filled with happiness and joyfulness, your eyes are closed. You're now a human astronaut flying through space. You're touching the moon and stars. At full speed, you're now past all the planets – Earth, Venus, Mercury, Mars, Jupiter, Saturn, Uranus, Neptune. You're flying past quicker than the speed of light.

Now you're a full blown fast-moving meteor. The light of flames is your power in your imagination. You're now an immortal object. Your body is now realistic. Your image is reshaped, unrealistic. You're going through millions and millions of time zones, circulating each planet around and around. You landed on the moon, you're dancing on the moon. You're now leaping and stepping on star after star. Slow, fast, or float or increase your speed. Seeing sparks everywhere, you start spinning around, in joy no more madness, no more sadness, no more badness, no more pain, only gladness. You own this now, you're the fastest.

You're powerful, you can now lift anything, throw any heavy thing, blow away any negative thing. It's now power in everything you do, it's electricity in everything you touch, your every touch is like a strike of lightning. Nothing or no one can stop you now. The moon looks at you and smiles. The stars dance with you whenever you dance. You don't need a spaceship, you don't need a space suit. You're surrounded by a powerful force field of electric light. No more darkness, rollercoasters of light zigzagging everywhere, here and there, all around. Beautiful colors of lights surround you, all around you.

You're now flying fast to meet the sun, you finally land on the sun, feeling its hot rays. You're already a powerful electric light. The sun is just a plug outlet. It will increase your faith, burn away all your doubts, and bring mental and physical healing. You're now like a piece of iron or metal, undentable, unbeatable, with the power of being invincible. Any negativity melts around you now. Hatefulness and jealousy go up in flames. The words poverty, joblessness, and lacking explode now, all burning in flames like a forest fire, never again to be heard of or mentioned. Struggling becomes tension, peacefulness is the new word for attention. We now think words like joy, happy, prosperity, longevity, good, love, abundance. Please! Always remember these words of hope.

When you see a beautiful rainbow on a humid day after a rainstorm, do these colors have any meaning? Which us as people can hold onto and live?

Red for enthusiasm, passion, security, vitality.
Orange for endurance, perseverance, and strength.
Yellow for cheerfulness, energy, and orderliness.
Green for growth, health, nature, and wealth.
Blue means calm, communication, knowledge, and peace.
Indigo for awareness and intuition.

Violet for creativity, imagination, luxury, mystery, and royalty.

Succeeding is our new goal platform, in all our hearts and spirits, we should all feel good about the meaning and what a rainbow of colors stand for. These meanings should give us more fight, more drive, more encouragement, more strive, more determination, mental inflation, for a new life creation, hopefully to educate the new generation, and let them see that there is hope towards a positive path, also let young people know that with negative thinking, they will not last, and that there is a choice between being good or bad.

Me and many people through the years have cried many, many tears. Some cried puddles and floods, some cried rivers, some cried lakes, we've all swam in them, floated in them, also drowned in them. Heavy tears like a rainstorm, light tears like drizzling, heavy drops, teary drops, streaks and streaks of dried tear lines down our cheeks because of sadness, emptiness, because of unhappiness, heartbroken, and because of madness. Pain after pain, your inner frame, pulling and carries the weight of a great train, trying to hold it all in, to keep from crying more tears of rain.

So you keep covered wearing dark shades to hide your eye redness, trying to cover your head and face with a hat, hoody, or scarf. No one can see your true hurt, they can't even try to imagine your outer and inner scarring, pain of piercing through your mind, body, and soul tearing along with your rainy tears. You may even scream loudly at times, when you're alone by yourself. From your struggles and downs in life, you don't smile anymore, you can't laugh anymore, you can't smirk anymore, or blush anymore.

You're hiding your pain really well, from the world, family, and friends can't even tell the hurt you're feeling, no more passion, maybe no more joy. Everything in your life seems to have crashed, and maybe you've even cashed in. Gave up on everything, gave up on everybody, gave up on life, gave up on hope, maybe you're not trying anymore. Change has taken so long, change has now become a non-existent word, a word you don't want to hear anymore. You're at a point in your life where you don't know what to do anymore, or who to turn to anymore, trust anymore, or what to believe anymore.

My advice is, maybe you're not around the right people, not talking to the right people, not getting good, helpful advice from the right people. Maybe you've been misled in some way. What type of folks have you been talking to? Or getting advice from? Good folks? Bad folks? If it's been bad folks, no wonder your beliefs, ideas, and thoughts are tangled up. You can change your mind and thoughts. Anyone in this world can change their own mind and thoughts. Getting around positive-thinking people, talking and hanging around with them, and most of all, listening to them will definitely change all your inner hurt, pain, and silly, doubtful thinking.

I've mentioned in my other book that in 1985, at age 13, I started writing rap rhymes. In the early to late 80s, I was inspired by storytelling rappers. Their rhymes were fun and funny, enjoyable to listen to. Those rappers were my role models. I wanted to cut my hair like them and dress like them. Rappers back then wore casual clothes, and some even wore suits and ties. Yes, of course, they sported their big thick gold chains and big gold rings. Their storytelling messages were about not growing up the way they did, staying in school, listening to your parents, staying out of the streets, not being stupid, and not being a fool because that isn't cool. Those were the messages they conveyed. I recall growing up as a teenager in the late 80s, listening to all the rappers back then, both male and female. Some may have been hippies or street-minded, hard or soft rappers, but all of them were positive rappers with positive messages.

Remember when becoming a rapper was all about feeling good, doing good, and being heard by the public with a positive voice? I'm still talking about the 80s here, but I'll touch on the 90s shortly. Even the R&B love songs back then had their charm. Rap music in the 80s made you want to do good, be good, and be a better person, both inside and out. It encouraged carrying a positive mindset and bopping your head to the beats of their music. I'm not going to name any specific rappers from the 80s, but you know who you are. If you made positive rap music aimed at steering the younger generation in a positive direction, you played an important role. Some rappers talked about not doing drugs and being smart, others about black power and having a militant mindset. There were songs about love or needing love, and some rappers even combined rapping with dancing. Others rapped about knowledge, and some female rappers made a statement with their stylish looks and makeup.

Switching conversations, I'm now talking about 80s R&B love music. Not all R&B music back then were love songs. Some R&B singers sang about wanting a decent woman who respects herself, a classy, sweet, sexy thing. Others sang about coming home from work to pay rent and buy clothes, or songs like "Make It Last Forever". Some R&B singers just talked about loving you with sexual lyrics, while other R&B love songs were about sad and bad relationships. The 80s black R&B was about love songs, a decade of love, how to respect a decent, good, fine-looking woman, and how to love her, appreciate her, and stay in love with her forever. There were certain love-slave-begging R&B soul singers, I won't mention any names, but they know who they are. Nowadays, in the millennium, you don't hear black love songs anymore. Those were the real fall in love times, the 80s. Now it's about big booty shaking, big booty banging, big booty jaw-dropping, big booty smacking, bent over big booty smashing, and pole hopping dancing. That's what's happening.

Now I will talk about rap music again. The 90s rap music, rap music and the rappers of this era, were somewhat struggling. Some of them were just trying to keep existing in the public eye of their fans. Rappers then had different style, skills, and opinions. Hairstyles became different, how they wore their clothes became different, street style like name brand. These new class of rappers were just trying to keep up the rap movement as it continued to change. Also, R&B soul music has changed. Now, the R&B era became about sex, hip-hop soul bumping, and grinding music. Rappers and R&B singers were showing no shame, just trying to maintain their fortune and fame, that was the name of the business game back then. Now let's fast forward quickly, up to date. Right now, rap music of today, has rap music become a blood sport? A blood sport arena, of who will be the last one standing, or maybe no one standing at all. So, the microphone and the recording studio have become deadly weapons, right?

Toward whoever has opposition, or for you if you have opposition, as today's rapper, their music beats are powerfully vibrating. It's addictive; you will bop your head up and down even if you don't agree with the lyrics. The beats move you, you can feel it, like skull candy headphones, the bass vibration can be felt deep in your bones, it can give a headache in your dome. Rappers today, 2022/23, are coming into the studio, male or female rappers, they're straight out of the street life, poverty, drugs, crime they've seen in their trenches, and I guess that's all they know and all they can rap about. Also, some rappers have opposition, other rappers whom they want to kill, and rappers who want to kill them, talking about their opposition and how many bodies they've dropped. I do understand poorness, poverty, and not having a father growing up, some rappers probably grew up without fathers, with no father figure in the home.

The Nigger from the Black Lagoon

I was also raised by a struggling single mother. A mother can't teach a son what his father can teach him. Maybe some rappers had a mother and a father, or a mother and no father, or a father and no mother. Maybe some rappers didn't have either parent in the home, perhaps one or both parents were on drugs. All of this, coupled with growing up in a poor poverty environment, is an explosion waiting to happen. So I guess maybe that's why rappers talk and say the bad things they say, including curse words. The hate inside of them is like poison. The taste of poverty, abandonment from a lack of a father made some feel they had to stand in a man's shoes at an early age, engaging in street activities like drug dealing, robbing, killing, or whatever. In the trenches, to them, rap was the only way out, no matter what they say in a recording booth. Believe me, I'm not sugarcoating anything. Rap music today, to me, has dangerous lyrics, and that's why so many rappers are dying young. The dangerous words in diss tracks and the actions behind the violent words have taken over.

Rap producers of today, do they even care about what the rapper is saying? Because they hear it first before the public, bad curse words, words of killing, words of anger and hate, a mad dangerous tone. Well, I know the rapper is paying for his or her recording time, oh the producer can't say nothing, right? Have a talk with a street rapper and just say hey bro, I'm feeling what you're saying bro, but can you tone it down a little? Don't talk so much about killing your opps and how you're gonna kill them, and bring down the curse words a little, oh okay, they can't? Or they aren't gonna say nothing? Maybe they're only thinking about their money flow, or is it just because they just plain scared to say anything because of the gun they might be carrying, too scared to tell that rapper hey bro I like working with you and producing your music bro, Please don't say nothing or diss anyone and get killed over that, please don't!

Maybe they might listen, maybe a caring way of talking will let that rapper know that at least one person cares about me and my life, or maybe they will even give it some thought. It probably just may take just a little talk like that to the rapper, they can say well at least my producer said he cares about me. Hey, a rapper's producer needs to step in and try that. Maybe these new upcoming rappers can stop dying so young. If that doesn't work, well the change needs to start somewhere. To all rappers that have babies and kids, your kids are looking at everything you do. You are their role model. You're a role model now to most young people, and most of you guys are millionaire rappers killing rappers. That's talent killing talent. It's a waste to die young, what a waste. It's sad to die period, at any age, but it's a waste to die young over pure silliness. So slack up and straighten up please!

See, I'm ordinary and plain. You gotta have a straight, positive mind with me if you want to hang. I don't bang bang, never been in a gang. My name is Shane, sounds strange. I don't play the blame game. You know right from wrong, we're all adults, different walks of life. Believe in your own hype. Believe you can switch the dice. Believe you're a big rat, not a mouse. Please, think twice before smoking the glass pipe. Stay positive, I know you want to live, even if you don't have much to give. It's okay to tremble and shiver every now and then. No, I don't own a Rolls Royce or Mercedes Benz. I don't have these things. I still believe I'm a ten. I won't blow over on the first or second wind. I'm solid like an oak tree, solid on my feet, no one can stray me from anything. I'm not simple-minded, believe that. You can't be, you won't be. We all are determined to conquer any challenges.

Sex feels so good, maybe lasts for about 30 minutes to 1 hour. How come something that feels so good as sex only lasts for a short time, but something that feels so bad lasts a lifetime or forever, like loved ones passing away, or a serious illness, racism, hatred, jealousy, evilness. Unfortunately, life is not forever, gee whiz, that's a bummer. My mother raised me in a bubble, some may say that, but I stayed out of trouble, I stayed humbled, I was isolated. She protected me from those who didn't care or love me, I avoided being violated, and that part of my mother I appreciated. And with no support, at 21, family called me a bum with 6 pair of pants. I hate that shit, I mean a bum, that shit. I was still determined to make it. I believed in my own self. That's every man's biggest prize or wealth. Keep scratching and clawing, believe one day you'll be standing tall. Even one day you'll be balling, because it's your calling. Hear what I'm saying, you all in, as I continue to write with this pad and pen, missing teeth I still grin.

See, when I was growing up as a young teenager, I was surrounded by a lot of prayer and spirituality. My mother and grandmother were both Pentecostal Christians, God rest their souls. Before I would go anywhere, my grandmother would pray for me, anointing my forehead and hands with olive oil, rubbing both hands and my forehead with prayer. I was hanging out in the streets, but I couldn't get involved in any kind of street activities, even if I wanted to, which I didn't anyway. It just wasn't in me to do that, and my friends couldn't influence or entice me either. I'm very, very glad I had prayer keeping me in a circle of protection back when I was growing up, even up to now. Those prayers were everlasting, still with me, and I'm proud of that. Most youngsters did not have prayer in their life growing up, so I'm forever grateful for that.

In 1984, at 12 years old, that was the year my mother first lost her mind, a nervous breakdown. I walked the streets of Brooklyn, New York, with her for 2 weeks, with no sleep. Yes, I ate during our street journey, but I was more concerned for her well-being, not mine, because she was hearing voices telling her something bad was going to happen to us both. And she already stated that something already has happened to the family, something bad. Also, she claims she was seeing rats climbing up her legs. Sounds funny, but it was sad, and a sad time for me. Everyone in the family was wondering what's happening to her and why. I was wondering the same thing. I was totally confused, but with her getting a lot of prayer and her taking her medications, her mind snapped out of it, in other words, back to normal thinking thoughts. Lord rest my mother Dolores's soul. She passed on June 29th at 6:44 am in ICU. She did admit that she had been one sick cookie. My mother had jokes.

Do you hate the race or culture you were born in? Do you hate your skin color, whether it's black, white, brown, dark, light, or jet black? Do you hate your hair, whether it's coarse, fine, curly, styled in cornrows, dreadlocks, wigs, or a toupee? Do you hate your face, your teeth, or the structure of your facial bones? Do you hate your smile or the shape of your legs, whether they're bow-legged, straight-legged, knock-kneed, splay-footed, or pigeon-toed? Maybe you dislike the way your feet look. Are they big, small, affected by athlete's foot, fungal infections, or do they have long, ugly, curved toenails? Do you hate your body shape, whether it's fat, skinny, nicely figured, disfigured, with parts bigger or smaller than others, uneven rolls, or perhaps you have no figure at all?

Okay, maybe you're one of those people who don't hate themselves. You love how you look, you love yourself, the shape of your body. You love and like your face, your hair, your skin color. Okay, maybe you adore your skin color, you adore every freaking thing about yourself. You've been told how good you look your entire life. Okay, you've had many compliments. You could never imagine how it would feel not to love or like yourself. To all the underdogs, low-esteem people, I know how you feel. My esteem is not always high also. I don't always love or like myself. I have to dig deep inside myself every single day, to find something in myself to keep my head lifted up. I've been an underdog before I became an author, and believe me, I'm still an underdog during my upbringing that's imprinted in my life. I've cried the same amount of tears you've cried so many times like you, so see, I do understand you and me.

To everyone, young and old, never ever listen to bad people or bad advice. Don't hang, walk, or talk with bad people because their life is bad, and they're doing bad. So, do you think those kinds of people have anything good to say to anyone about anything? Think. Surround yourself only with good, positive-thinking people. They can't and won't steer you in the wrong path or direction. Sadly, most positive people are in high positions in life, and you might still get stepped on or looked down on. I worked at SPPLUS parking garage, Bronx NY, from 2015-2021. I was a parking attendant, only making $15/hr. There was a 6 feet 3 tall black court judge who used to come into the garage, my place of work, he and his wife, she looked like she had a good-paying job also. They both would come in, and neither of them ever spoke to me, and they had been coming to the garage the same time I've been working there. They would look at me and didn't say good morning or anything. I guess they thought, well, if that attendant doesn't speak to us first, well, we sure ain't because we're above him, and he's beneath us. We both have better jobs than he does, and we make a whole lot more than him and his coworkers, monthly and yearly. So therefore, they never spoke to me, and I never spoke to them, period. I didn't give a shit how much more money they made than me or their good job position. Man, forget all those people that parked in that garage with their good jobs, forget all of them. Sorry, everyone, I had to get that off my chest. It's okay to go off every now and then. I say let it out because it's not easy being stepped on and looked down. I know, anyway.

The Nigger from the Black Lagoon

On Sunday going into Monday morning, November 20th and 21st, 2022, during Thanksgiving week, I traveled with Greyhound bus services. I live in Fort Walton Beach, Florida, and was going to Atlanta, Georgia, for the Thanksgiving holiday. At Montgomery, Alabama, bus terminal, where many travelers at all of the gates were going away for the holiday, I was at gate 3, waiting to go to Atlanta. Also, gate 2 was going to Atlanta. Well, the most unfortunate thing happened. Gate 2 boarded first, then gate 3, where I was standing, boarded. By the time the gate 3 line I was in boarded, there were no empty seats left on the bus. A bus full of black people from different states, cities. Nobody offered me any seat. People were taking up two seats with their feet and bags. There was one young black dude who also had his bag in the other seat. Well, he saw me coming to the back of the bus where he was sitting. Well, he pretended to be asleep when he was just awake looking at me coming because I was looking right at him as he looked at me.

And that bus driver was no help at all. He did nothing but walk through the bus aisle and said to me, "People paid for one seat, not two seats. Go in and sit or stay and wait for the next bus," which he said wouldn't come until the next day. So, I guess he didn't care. Once again, I entered the bus, and everyone was staring at me like I was crazy. This heavy-set girl slightly opened up her heart, but before that, she also had her bag in the aisle seat. So, I sat down next to her and said I'm sorry and appreciate it. By me appreciating that seat, that seat became a nightmare. We both were big-sized, but luckily she didn't miss any of her sleep and she seemed comfortable, unlike me. I was leaning over, almost off my seat, sitting on one side of my seat. I couldn't relax or go to sleep at all.

See, this is an example of black people not loving, caring for, or sharing with each other. Anyone on that full Greyhound bus could have said, "Hey brother, hey mister, or even yo, come sit next to me," but they didn't. Now, I'm not saying I'm an elderly man, or even much of an old man, but I'm not a young man either, and I did deserve to sit, no questions asked. Like I mentioned, I did sit, but that seat was a nightmare beyond nightmares. I probably would rather sit my ass on a large fish tank with piranhas in it because that seat was causing me so much pain in my behind and legs.

My behind was hurting, my legs were hurting and cramping as well as my right foot and legs going to sleep. I was just looking at my watch, looking at the roads, and hoping to see some ATL signs for miles and miles, road after road, distance after distance. I was asking God to please help me get through this night of horror traveling. Well, after this, I give Greyhound services on a scale of 1-10, I give it a 1. Whoever is flying Southwest, Spirit, Delta, even Frontier Airlines, please keep flying to all travelers.

I could have said "I'm a book writer and author, can I use or have this seat?" If it's okay, I really don't think saying that would have made a damn difference. Well, I wonder, would it have been different if the bus was full of white people? Would I have gotten a seat without any doubt or hesitation? Or possibly the same result, I don't know. Believe me, backlashes can come from your own race of people first, rawness, hatefulness, wickedness, evilness towards you. Every race, creed, or color has their good and bad points, faults, and downfalls, but see, at the end of the day, goodness, doing what's right has to be in your heart. Therefore, you can't do any good deeds or do the right thing. All people need to change, but black people really need to change, change the hatred and evilness they have for each other.

Although I'm an author and a book writer, why do I still walk with my head hung down and feel empty sometimes, feeling lonely sometimes, feeling alone sometimes, feeling rejected? Through Dorrance Publishing, my writing talent was selected, and I'm so grateful. My work was accepted, my writing finally paid off, through my years of being neglected. And although I'm a lucky bastard, a man that grew up with a mother and no father, the word "bastard" is because I never had a father, the word "lucky" is because I've been blessed to have this wonderful writing talent. At an early age of 13 in 1985, 37 years of writing, memorizing, using a pad and pen without any typing, my manuscript is my loud voice, my input chip. Like a loud bass drum instrument, my words I'm writing are permanent, and to me, that was excellent.

If I had many wishes, my main wish is to continue my education and try to earn a GED. I have 12th-grade knowledge, but I didn't receive a high school diploma. I was dealing with a lot of obstacles growing up, and I guess those obstacles have gotten the best of me. Not having a high school diploma is the biggest missing piece of my life. Let me correct that, the biggest missing piece in my life is when my mother passed away in ICU on June 29, 2014, from a massive bleeding brain stroke; she died in a coma. Not having a high school diploma is my second missing piece. This is a past old goal that I would still like to accomplish. There are certain things in life that make a person's life incomplete, regardless of how old you may be, there's always something that you feel inside that there's more to be done, and therefore, yes, there are uncompleted things in my life. Getting a GED diploma and meeting a nice decent woman, she doesn't even have to be pretty, but if so, ok, whatever these 2 requests in my life need to be completed.

To all Black people, put the alcohol bottle down, stop using drugs, be a man, be a woman, be a better mother, be a better father, be a better sister, be a better brother, better uncle, better nephew, better grandmother, better grandfather, be a better husband, a better wife, better cousin, be a better friend. White people, all people, race, creed, or color, if you need to make any kind of changes in your life, make it. People, change is in the air, everywhere, here, over there. Stop! Take time to breathe in and exhale. The choice is ours, every minute, every hour. Don't let what I'm saying to you blow away in the wind like powder.

A mother is a mother, and a father is a father. Both have the same meaning. A mother is another who was there for her child or children, all from birth through that child's youth up to adulthood. That's a mother, but we all know mothers are the only ones left raising that child or those children all by themselves, without a husband or the father of her child or children being part of their life. No, a father is a father, and it has the same meaning, being there for that child or children, from that child's birth, youth, until adulthood, and a majority of so-called fathers hit and run, and are never there, or part of that child or children's life, so their absent name is that man. As far as me, I was raised by a single mother, and my late mother named Delores Williams, that man was supposed to have been there. The last time I saw that man was when I was in the hospital at age 14 in 1987 in children's ICU from a ruptured appendix. Thank God for His love and mercy, for working through that old Chinese man's hand to operate on me to remove that right side hernia. I thank God for keeping me alive. That man came in the room, we've talked a bit, and he exited just giving $20.00. Now before 1987 at 14 years old, I have not seen that man since 1979 at age 7. I remember when that man came and took me shopping for a light blue suit, 3 pieces, and some other clothes. Well, you look at the time between those years, of me not having a father, and the years my dear mother had to raise me all by herself, on welfare of course like so many other poor Black and minority kids. Now my mother did have odd jobs every now and then, but she still had to turn to welfare from time to time. 1979 age 7, when Michael Jackson's album first came out "Off the Wall" album, I remember the songs "Rock with You" and "Don't Stop 'Til You Get Enough." Wow, well 1989, I heard that that man met and married another woman and they had a daughter which will be my half-sister, at some point in time and I hope to meet her one day. Also, I heard that that man had a New York City bus driving job and a city job as we all know, makes good money, so it's a shame that that man wasn't there for me. Well, I'm 50 years old now and a child or children need both a mother and a father involved in their life.

Racism still exists because I've faced it many times in New York City. I had white people see me coming down the same side of the street and they literally crossed to the other side of the street. Or maybe an old white couple will come out when they see a black man about to enter the elevator, and if they do happen to find the courage to stay in the elevator with a black man, they would have to stand there facing you, not turned around with their back to you, oh no way, no how.

Or an old white woman may grip her pocketbook or purse real tight, close to her when she sees me coming past her, and most of the time these events were taking place, I was in a working uniform. Well, June 22nd, 2022, last year, I moved out of the rotten big apple "aka" city of dungeons and dragons, crime, rapists, killers, robbers, crack addicts, drug dealers, child molesters. MTA bus service, MTA underground train service, crime has run rapidly through that hellhole, but I left NYC Harlem then moved to Fort Walton Beach, Florida, for the low crime rate and very high racist rate. I'm so sorry to say that, but the truth shall set you free and God knows I'm telling the truth. I faced more racism in Fort Walton Beach, Florida, in one year than I faced in New York in my entire life, and I was born and raised there.

People in Fort Walton Beach, Florida, are cruel, some are friendly, but others are either mad or have a racist attitude. I went to the emergency room at HCA Fort Walton Beach Destin Hospital, and it was for mild off on heart palpitations because of a certain medication I was taking, but anyway, the young male white doctor talked to me in an angry voice, a voice not caring, a voice of racism, a voice of madness and hatred. One morning I was riding my electric bike facing oncoming traffic I was only trying to get to the bike lane, and I saw the Okaloosa County vehicle in front blocking me, and the young white sheriff yelled out in an angry, disrespectful on his loudspeaker "You're going against the traffic, move to the other side of the street right now." I'm an old man, well not that old, but I'm old with gray hair and old enough to be his father if I was white but that's not how a law officer is supposed to talk to a person, and I told him that I just moved here, I'm just trying to learn the streets.

Going in and out of Sam's Club in Fort Walton Beach, FL, many times I would just be in there looking around, walking around, walking down the aisles. I noticed white people moving away from me, moving away from around me, and moving out of the aisles. Living in this place, Fort Walton Beach, Florida, I was never shown any kindness. This one year of moving out of New York, I've only been dealing with racist attitudes and racist people that have fake smiles and fake handshakes. Racism is a wolf in sheep's clothing, also bigotry. Is getting slapped or punched in the face worse than racism and bigotry? No, I don't think so, racism and bigotry hurt more. Racism and bigotry are not something you can see; you feel it, also inside. Yes, a feeling you get inside, and it's a bad feeling.

As I was nicely escorted out, it seemed to me like I was kicked out of Hyundai Car Dealership in Fort Walton Beach, FL, located on Hollywood Blvd and Memorial. And just to think, the white lady that kicked me out, I gave a free copy of my book "Grey Hairs in the Mirror," and I even signed it for her. But that didn't make a damn difference. Have you ever heard of an author being thrown out of a car dealership place? Yes, if that author is black. And this white guy came out to try to make up a story. But I asked him, was this a race thing? He paused, then said no, we serve all people. That's bull shit! To me, I felt disrespected; it's all because I came through their car lot with my 49cc scooter looking for a car to purchase. Since I've been waiting on the money, which was taking days and weeks, so every day or every other day I'll come in with my scooter through their parking lot, and they also saw me roll out. They still didn't have anything I liked, so I went to the next car dealership, and the young white lady even laughed and picked on my scooter. This has been one racist whip of many that I received in Fort Walton Beach, FL.

This is modernized racism, where people give you a phony smile and phony handshakes, also a phony speech. Racism is a wolf in sheep's clothing. These people who wear this face don't like you or your skin color. They are tolerating and dealing with you because you're part of this world and society, and they know that you aren't going anywhere, so they are forced to deal with you and your race of people, although they hate it. And often, they prove that they hate you by shooting up a shopping mall, shopping store, hospital, movie theater, or a school, pharmacy, or out in the open street. Hatred of others makes them shoot up places, with an AR-15 rifle or whatever other weapon they desire to use.

Oh Lord, through many years of struggle, my life has seemed to be broken, in millions of pieces like a puzzle. I still search and seek, inside of me, day by day, night by night for inner peace, and trying to constantly find the strength to keep standing up on both feet. Although I'm an author, which is a wonderful talent to me, there are days I still cry and weep, walking with my head hung down, with my heart fallen to my feet. No one is too old to groan, to shed a tear, or shiver and have fear. Life is precious, timeless, we are mortal, vulnerable, born into this world, mindless and blindness, from the cradle to the grave. Only God can grant longevity and abundance, yes God, and His Son Jesus is our landlord. All us people are just earthly tenants in this world, we are renters of life, and just like a lease, we're given a certain amount of time, and we all know what happens when the lease runs out, right?

As long as God continues to let us live, let's walk and stay encouraged, not discouraged, walk with our armor vest on, and chest standing out, without any doubt. The joy in our hearts will make us scream and shout. Everyone's joyful voices can be heard, north, east, west, and south. Believing, achieving is what it's all about. Walking tall, standing tall, don't let no one below you, down you, talk down to you, think they're better than you, regardless of how educated they are, how smart they are, how rich they are, or how many earthly possessions they have. They may have more than you, maybe they have it all. Every man is born into this world with nothing, and every man will leave this world with nothing, that's God's holy words. So does it matter? No high-minded man is immortal, rich or poor. Life is fragile and easily shattered.

Thank you for reading. Remember to keep your head held up high and stay encouraged, no matter what tough situation you may be in and regardless of all the crazy things going on in this world right now, like all these senseless shootings going on across 52 cities and states. Let's all stay encouraged, and be careful. I'm giving a shout out to my remaining living relatives, Aunt Shalaunda, cousin Jeremy, and to the rest of the family, and I'm sending my love to my family members who passed away. I wish you all are still here, continue to rest in God's peace! Bye bye everyone and stay safe!